ON THE WAY TO JERSUALEM FARM

Carola Luther's first two collections, *Walking the Animals* (2004) and *Arguing with Malarchy* (2011) were published by Carcanet Press. *Walking the Animals* was shortlisted for the Forward Prize for First Collection. *Herd*, a pamphlet of poems, was published by The Wordsworth Trust where Carola was Poet in Residence in 2012. She was born in South Africa but now lives in the Calder Valley, West Yorkshire.

ALSO BY CAROLA LUTHER FROM CARCANET

Arguing with Malarchy (2011)
Walking the Animals (2004)

On the Way to Jerusalem Farm

CAROLA LUTHER

CARCANET POETRY

First published in Great Britain in 2021 by
Carcanet
Alliance House, 30 Cross Street
Manchester, M2 7AQ
www.carcanet.co.uk

A CIP catalogue record for this book is
available from the British Library.

ISBN 978 1 80017 163 3

Book design by Andrew Latimer
Printed in Great Britain by SRP Ltd, Exeter, Devon

The publisher acknowledges financial
assistance from Arts Council England.

CONTENTS

Possibility of Horses

ON THE WAY TO JERUSALEM FARM

CAMPFIRE

      how the cattle
      move across the sun-scorched field
      like marquees of Hannibal how the cattle
lower their heads to water touched
by floating summer powder how the cattle
leave their muzzles floating there
      as if they too are seeds or dust as if
      they wait not quite
      to drink but to absorb the other
trance-eyed cow they nuzzle nose to nose
and the water how the cattle osmose
drowsiness a déjà vu of
      twilight from the trough
      while the water level in it
      drops
and drops how the cattle turn back across
the hot cropped field
to pitch their tents around the grass edge
      as if these last green flames
      are campfire and tomorrow
      they'll be gone

LETTERS TO RASOOL

ON FLIGHT

There are still planes Rasool

Day and night they stack

      flock

  I saw one tilt
        all alone
like memory   of hawk
            or albatross

Airports remain
airports

        Do you recall
        the possibility   risk

no mans land
biometric passports
sterile air
      clocked
            unclocked
and not a wild thing
to care about

Today I buy an old-world map
Every flattened country
every coast

Rasool I have a hunch where you may be
Each time I land
I'll make my way down to the sea

ON FINDING THE WAY

Now I've turned the corner
I can see her Rasool
      the architect of sands gazing at her small city
      It looks Moroccan
      and not just because it's the colour of lions

This beach might be my longing
or yours   but this morning I woke on it
face down
      The tide had receded
      and the sand beneath me was cold and hard

Standing   I saw no dog   no bird
      no woman or man
and from the flat sea which could have been mercury
nothing breached
      no rock or whale-spout or hoop
      of dolphin   not even a fibreglass boat

I recalled no-one had seen fish for decades

I miss you Rasool

I started to compose a prayer
             It was difficult   The art of it
struck me as more important than I could understand
And in my search to pinpoint the precise keen-tone
to mourn for sand-fleas and molluscs
I found myself on my knees
marvelling at minutiae of quartz and sea-rubbed plastic
and it was then that I saw them

> A sandpiper's footprints
> so faint   from certain angles
I lost them in light

And I remembered how shorebirds
used to run between waves
>   and on their way in
>   and on their way out
the waves did not always
wash away imprints

three wire toes   arrow
>   after arrow   pointing
to where the bird had run from
>   where I should go

Who would not weep Rasool

I followed directions and turned back   walked east
>   around the headlands

>   And now I can see her
>   her white shirt flapping
>   in the crook of the bay

She is crouching down
brown hands at work on her next suburb
>   I imagine small arched windows
>   walls bleached pale
>   almost pink
>   like shells
>   or salt-pan camels

ON FAITH

At the resort a woman told me of a turtle
glimpsed under torchlight on the coast of Oman
       She had seen it as a child Rasool
         laying its eggs in the sand
Her father in his white thaub
let go of her hand and knelt
in the night's heat and whispered
a message to the turtle
                 Or a song
                         Or a hamd

       For the turtle's faith he had said
       tears silvering his face
       in the moonlight

The story she told
was a full bowl held
       Our faces swayed in its water

Inside me   a voice like a pin
       Not faith
       Instinct

And I imagined you laughing   saying again
Pray   what is the difference

So I linked arms with the woman and we walked on
through dunes
       listening to the sough
       and the silence

ON IMPERMANENCE

Last night Rasool I dreamed
not of the sea
        but of the Wild Grass Parade

Wade with me I said
into summer grass
Come in close
            magnify
            binocule
            microscope

And there we are
as we used to be
        little stalks
                carnival city

                frill feather fur-
                below
                buffy fluffy
                green drag frocks

all the swanny greeny necks

bent

                                        fec-

cund   fec-

cund

                the weight of lace

a young summer king's

edifice

heavy droopy
        ten-tier gauzy
                loaded wispy
                        sugar-icing
                                wedding cake

your fascinator   shiver quiver

        my beau chapeau   shakey quakey

them in pinky gaudery
them in lettuce-hem trousseaux

Then ears of common bent
hear the meadows scream
      Is it Columbine   No
a tractor turning in

COM   BINE
COM   BINE
COM   BINE

Oh Rasool the déshabillé
your applique's
unstuck
my eyelash slips
your tulle's reduced to sticky mesh
quick trim up
sway

swish
make a stand
      this is our
            yellowgreen   our
field of summer

Look you say
there goes Demeter
      running
        running

COM   BINE

It's time to raise our superstructure headgear   now
   Fling and flaunt our paper beads   now
      Send our little capsules of tomorrow   out   out
         into another year
           with the whole
               roaring   falling   tiara-tossing crowd

Any minute now

Rasool I bow and doff my fandangle-tufted hat to you

You say   *Our days my darling*
          are as grass

ON BLOSSOM (I)

Fret Rasool
settles on the shore   The misery
which covers up and will not change
I hear you say *Underneath something grows*

How long did you believe

I've feared for you
sometimes imagined your box of light
scroll of sofa
while here   I stumble on in fog

But last night Rasool
I saw the sewer had brought forth
          a flowering thing
If I could   I'd have sent you a telegram
          Jellied frill stop
          Galgalim stop
          Amalgam of phosphorescent
          passionflower and amphibian
          come soon
stop
          I want to tell you
how it sucked its stamen
with a sphinctral *pock*
see you ache with laughter

Does it
you would ask   *have sticky carmine lips*
Rasool   I would answer   *not blossom*
as we know it   *but yea*
          an efflorescence

ON GIANTS

Last week I lost the map Rasool
    Seaside people helped me search the sand
A woman whistled *Molly Malone sweet Molly Malone*
    and I returned to that pale morning

                You and I
                balanced
                on basalt columns
                pretending to be giants
                 yelling
                      alive alive oh
                          to our stone twins
                          over the sea

Last week I lost the map
    Rasool   seaside people helped me search
The sand   a woman   whistled *Molly Malone Sweet Molly*
    Malone and I returned to that pale morning

                You and I
                balanced on basalt
                      Columns pretending
              to be
                    Giants yell *Alive*
                    Alive
                      Oh our stone twins
                      over the sea

Last week I lost   The map Rasool   Seaside
   People helped me search   The sand woman whistled
Molly Malone sweet Molly Malone and I
       Return to that pale morning

          You
          and I balanced
          Basalt columns
            Pretend giants
          yelling
            alive alive oh
          to our stone
               Twins over the sea

ON MEMORY

Rasool I haven't seen a seal
for twenty years
There are gene-banks and archives
but what do they mean
People recorded leviathans
griffins
the fauns of Pan

That day we were told
self is more tile
          than galaxy or planet
I still smile at your retort
          Thank God for mosaics

They say we remember what's been
remembered before
          photographs   stories   videos
Who knows what's true

The other day
I recalled your sea-clean toes
pointing to the sky

Was that the time
the canoe ran aground

                              spit
                              sandbar
                              tiny island

The sense is mostly in my gullet and bones
how consoling it was to lie down
and face the sky
            its slow cuneiform of gulls

We could have been Henry II and Eleanor of Aquitaine
      you holding the paddle to your chest
            me clutching my mobile phone

It was good Rasool   to stare into blue
that didn't move and
gaze along our length to the sand-stippled crust
half-shoeing our toes

            Or were our toes clean

I know we did play a game

You seabed
I fundus
you isthmus
me dune
you bluff and skerry and headland
me wave-cut platform
These words pool on my tongue

But not the sounds
                  seals
that called to us over the bay
            their barks
                  and lullings
                        and mewing questions

Rasool   did we sing to the seals
or to each other as we paddled home
I imagine sirens
        selkies   sea-ghost cries
            But they aren't memories

Rasool I don't remember the journey home

ON BLOSSOM (II)

This morning my thoughts returned to that hot city
running through percussing streets
the escape
from government tank
how we dropped   legs gone
retching for air on the pitted road

The town's last street
We were insects on our backs in that slab of shade
      Beyond
            the desert edge
transparent ocean we would wade out in   out and out
till we disappeared
part of the disturbance   flecks
of asbestos dust

            It'll be alright you said

In the tarmac cracks
you found six cotyledons
downy as newborn puppy ears
Bowing low   you offered three to me   palm
a cup   *Dandelion your Highness*
   For the thirst

I laughed   and now I smile again
Dandelion   no

more like devils-snare or puncture-vine
but thanks Rasool
          I don't think I ever thanked you
those leaves were sweet and moist on my tongue

And nowadays I find I name any
little leaf   *dandelion*
see it as libation of a kind
flag of hope

ON DESPAIR

Rasool I watch the drowning sun
lay its orange column
over the bay again

Tomorrow I move on
I've tried to imagine the journeys made
whether you've come or gone

or tried to return   All conjecture
So let me tell you about the wheatear
It landed last month on the harbour wall

Grey crown   yellow neck
Did not respond to coaxing
Hopped   took off

was chased down streets
this *Old World Flycatcher*
eluding the crowd

as if all dreamt San Fermin
the forgotten
running of the bulls

The bird succumbed
was scooped up by a girl
and displayed in the skylit

vestibule of City Hall
Outside we watched onscreen
Clips of it   Humanely caged

with background birdsong   adverts
news bulletins   A caretaker
was required to keep watch each night

the bird beating at bars
instinct   or was it faith
propelling wings

the reaching forward of its heart
The caretaker broke its neck
Compass cracked

Locked up for life
History of the world
in a grain of sand

ON BLOSSOM (III)

We aimed for the hump of rocks
Why there   I don't recall
Perhaps the shape reminded us of dolphin pods

Our powdered brows and lashes   legs thorned
with desert salt   The good luck
terrorists we met   their watchful eyes
corners of warm water
offered from a carrier bag

The child who asked to call her mother
from our one bar phone
The dappled sister pointing the only way
through the canyon   Rasool

I am sorry for the arguments
when thirst kicked in   How I mocked
you lizarding at sound of drone or plane
But you did call me cactus   locust
stone

And I hissed   You sneered
I pelted you with sand   and you erupted
with desert sores
me with sunburn

Do you remember how we reached the shore
I see coral brittles
helmets   empty foilpacks
of ketamine
burned out vehicles

And the rock pool   *Look*
you said   *Blossom*
There beside the floating cartridge cases
of someone's enemy
a dancing purple-green anemone

ON GHOSTS

Yesterday it wasn't so   but today there is sadness
in this sea-city   A concavity
like the small cleft that thumbs remember
between the wishbones of birds
Last week I found a washed-up bird Rasool
still as a stopped clock
empty on the inside   feathers
stiff with salt

Today a man stands on the promenade
staring out to sea   At this hour
if there was work
he'd be there

The couple on the bench have someone huge
missing between them   A child
clad in rockets passes by
with a woman employed by his mother
The woman's mind is not on the child
The child rams the bin with a missile
The woman too is a mother   no time off
till next year   no credit
to go   and in another country
her own boy
about to emerge from his chrysalis

On the pavement a running man
He'd remind me of you Rasool
except for the crossbones
At the playground he comes to a stop   Looks up
We all look up   Even the couple
tilt faces like radars searching for daytime meteors

I could swear what we heard was a seagull
crying   *now*

        now   *now*

              now

Then the child begins again to pound the balustrade
and all there is
is the sky's damp glove
pressing down on the mountain
Otherwise nothing Rasool
Nothing

ON STARLINGS

My dear Rasool
I'm tired today
      Snow like pixels on this northern beach
      Sand is black
      Someone has balanced
pebbles on a rock
two stone figures
staring out to sea
They almost touch
They seem to watch the hanging snow
          as if the snow
          might be alive
as if the snow
could be a bird   no
          is myriads of seabirds
          kittiwakes
beating in from east and south
to relearn memory

      murmuration

in the absence of crows
in the absence of starlings

Rasool I think I'll stay here for the winter

FALLING THROUGH AIR

MORNING BIRDS

Again, there is someone when I wake.
I say your name,
remember you are away,
feel the cool body
of absence beside me.

                    Tin tin tin says the morning bird

Figures in the shapes of empty clothes:
bishop defeated in the gown
behind my half-open door,
crouching builder
working on a low wall,
stranger staring from the hood-up
hood hung on the bannister,
all sinister, all silent, all waiting,
and when I switch on the light,
vanishing.

              Tweak tweak twarr
              tweak tweak twarr says the morning bird
              swinging cheerily on the old telephone wire
              (is it still called a telephone wire
              these days?) *Who knows bébé*
              says the morning bird, *bébé*
              who cares?

Not the dead who have come
with their powdery hands. Nor the trickier
visitors, hammering at all hours

Clear your cookies cookie,
says the morning bird. I will remember
to tell the children, before its too late.
(*Huh* the children will snort,
I can hear them now
full of sky and sweet contempt)

Tring tring bright day bright
says a gaudy fowl *Good morning good morning
wake up call darling
your wake up call*

and in the distance
its sour cousin *Eight days lady
just eight*

Fading
almost-shapes –
something forgotten I must remember
from the peopled night

*Eight days lady
            just eight days lady
            eight*

                                    *

Party-line phones,
their turning handles,
two *shorts*, one *long,*

            (brp brp brrrp)

bushfire
murder
the butcher's order
hornets in the thatch of the church

Pass it on, call England,
the exchange-lady saying
ag sorry skattie, trunk-lines are down,
cut off, cut off
ja-nee, kommunikasie vandag
is vir die birds

Girl, don't be a fool.
What good are *voëls* as messengers,
with their own morning jokers and naysayers,
their wayward flirts, and skivers,
their tricksters in any language –
            though that swallow on the wire
might have news if you could decipher it,
harbinger of sorts,
almost prophet
not what's said but between it

                Listen to this
Listen to this   prrray
        not that   this
Listen   listen to this   this this this
listen   listen
        prrray
prrray

THE FUGITIVES

We stumble from the forest
spruce at our backs, minatory and dark

as an unknown police force.
We find a path, but it winds up at a quarry –

could be our bombed street.
You panic at the rock

but the sun comes out, and we see
blue swirls in the granite,

atolls of lichen ochreing light.
New grass nestles our feet

and the grass smells like ghee
after days of deprivation.

I say *In this handkerchief of meadow*
between quarry and hectares

of government pine,
here old love, shall we rest? I see you drink in

a place that has everything anyone might need,
its hiatus of sunlight

we could name as our own. *Let's sit*
I say, before you begin to cry again. *No* –

let's doze, allow ourselves
one small summer.

So we lie in our bodies
and are silent.

Then you say *wild flowers*
like bright clothed shoppers.

And I say, *shifty willow,*
hopeful birch.

And you say *clouds*
like ruminants – no –

like neighbours. Joggers.
Market-stall holders. Jacketed people

walking normally to work in sun. People in rush-hour traffic
taking children to school, like children at school – like –

And I say *hush now, darling.*
Hush. Don't let's talk.

After a while you sleep,
your breath a small animal in undergrowth

transporting seeds, and I feel the span of seconds
widen immeasurably, forget

buildings that staggered to their knees, the hanging
rooms, the shells exploding. Birdsong

today is a million
minuscule bells falling

and falling through air, and air
is a bowl of God so deep and blue

I never do hear the small bells land.
And through my eyelashes

I watch mayflies like Sufis
ecstatically spinning above a makeshift pond,

a ten-day puddle really, filled
with Spring rain.

A water lily leaf
unrolls a boat there

three reeds becoming
the oar of its dream.

PENDING ASYLUM

I fall into the hole of where I stay.
Each night it waits for me. That first winter
I saw the pretty frost from the inside
trying out bones.

Now it is summer I watch legs and shoes passing,
flies to-ing and fro-ing across the deep-set window.
I like to pretend the flies are apricot bees.

The bees in my mind have made it
across an orchard of almonds
still standing, round cumulus dust and smoke,
past blocks of flats cracked open like hives,
through scars in the sky, the eight-year war, summer,
winter, summer, and over
the ossuary sea. Exhausted they hum
like the engine room
of the last heroic
whale shark.

I feel for them all: the bees, the fish, the flies,
sometimes the unknown faces that belong
to this city's legs.

In the evenings I fill an old tin bath.
I look down at the seas of the world
and wish I had a sister.
My precarious brothers struggle in their own boats
and would not want to know of this mayhem.
Waves tonight are higher than anyone could have expected.
I lean close-up. The indrawn breath

between each wave reaching its tip
and its turn, goes on longer
than anyone could have expected.
The triumph of weight
feels like relief.

Tonight, flies cool on the windowsill.
They may see the streetlight. Everyone needs to believe
there's a moon. I reflect on two things.
Was tension the template for breath and
elastic, and is collapse easier always
than standing upright?
I pray for the sharks and bees
and then begin shouting loudly
my unpronounceable name.

COMMERCE, MADRID, 2012

All afternoon the geese fly over the city. Women
in twos, waiting for men beside municipal trees.
Shopping continues. The sore sweet
rut of it. We watch traffic, like tourists.

All afternoon the geese fly west over the city, hauling
wakes behind them in strings and waves. Women
stand, disappear, emerge. It's cold. Under glass
we hold hot Spanish chocolate. Shopping continues.

All afternoon labouring geese fly over the city. Cars hoot,
sirens fugue. Beneath bank towers, a statue shifts. A man,
blue clown, blows two-note whistles for a living.
Shopping continues. New women arrive. Others stay

and stay. Geese heave their huge hearts over the city,
the sky a stitched membrane that will hold for a day.
We watch the day end, blood orange. Men come, women
return. Shopping continues. Under lit trees, women in twos.

GREYLAG

Get out my way
out the way
gaan gaan gaan
get out
out the way   out
        got to get out
        gaan gaan
get out the way
get out *gaan*
got to get out
got to get out
        vandaag   today

        veranderen
            veranderen
          verander
     veranderen
veranderen

KESTREL

Lift
Luft
Loft
      Aloft
Air
*Lug/*Air
*Lug/*Air
Lig
      *Lug/*Air
Look
Luch
Lock

Drop

WREN

roitelet/
        dreoilin/
   wren   your song liquid
                           sugar
on my tongue   *elan*
                chi
     chi   *chi*
  chi-chi-churro-chi-chi-chi

MAGPIE

Unguarded   once a *yes*
squeaked out
despite the strut   the natty suit
of black and white

Its usual call
glottle
guttural   machine-gun imitation
n- n-n-n-n-n-n-n-n

Variation
krrr krrr   cold-world-
rattlesnake or
krrr krrr   cold-war-
agent   *nyet*   double-
agent
transmitting lies   or could it be
the truth *da –*

nyet   *nyet*   *nyet*   *nyet*

August hauls deep green dreaming
into the woods.
Even the bracken is so high and thick
I am up to my neck.
I feel its lure -
who doesn't desire to trust
in what's sprung, the emerald
caves, to lean in and be lost.

Clouds. Someone calling
their dog. Just here, I could be
in the clefts of Magoebaskloof
no, more Lekgalameetse, (called *Malta*
then, and *The Downs*). Trees hang
heavy, comatose with their own
inner workings, there are vines
hanging like boomslangs. I imagine

flashes – grenadilla, snare, hungry man
and a silent blue swordtail butterfly
blinking the eyes of this upturned
cauldron of leaves. I find the towpath.
Me, three ducks and the white
disturbance of that eight-foot swan-
shaped paddleboat stowed amongst nettles
on the opposite bank.

I can't see the rain,
but can see it's raining –
the green water receives it
with tiny pale mouths, fish lips

pulling down rain. Narrowboat
framed by the bridge. It's come on
so quietly. From nowhere
the thought that it's Stalkie inside,

Stalkie pulled straight
like a king laid out on a slab, kill-wounds
filled in and powdered by curators
of the dead. A hooded man
at the tiller staring ahead,
poncho beaded with rain.
I realise this myth is European.
It isn't actually Stalkie in my mind,

I don't know Stalkie now,
did he have guns, I hear
he was a peaceful man, but a farmer
will have a gun. I don't think of his killers,
I don't, they may have been desperate,
I heard they were from Mozambique
and had taken drugs, *for courage* my brother
thought, breaking bones like they couldn't

stop, and Stalkie, I haven't seen Stalkie
for forty years. Square-shouldered boy
racing bare-foot with my bare-foot
brother, freckle-face, snub nose,
pocket full of goons, his tiny mother
teaching us to swim, big bosom
making bird-breast of her costume,
she died last year –

Thank God for that my brother said. Her sister
grew northern hemisphere azaleas,
maples from America, acres
of European cherry blossom,
you remember the blossom
my brother said. I remember
standing ankle deep in light
petals cooling my feet.

In this boat is Stalkie, metaphor
for a world that once I knew
here, in another country, this water
a Styx, a momentary Charon in the rained-on
Yorkshireman at the narrowboat tiller.
The man nods. I lift my arm
walk on quickly to Luddenden Foot,
turn up to Jerusalem Farm.

BETWEEN VISITS

BIRTHDAY AT EMILY COURT

for Olwen

Hip hip Noreen,
hip hip…

*

Now we have sung, and made our toasts with pop and beer
through the leaves, through the window, light like water

we gather round tables with friends and strangers, making time
for the old folk, letting small-talk darn us in for the afternoon.

And Grace, Noreen's friend, who'd been sitting alone, *light like water*
running over her tells me she'd been left by her husband, her children's father

at the age of seventy-one. She went out she said, and bought sand,
trowel, gravel, bags of cement, *running leaves making patterns*

like light on water and transported slab after slab of sandstone, Indian,
similar to Yorkshire but with a rosy tinge, and with ungloved hands

laid down flags for a patio - he'd always promised a patio – shuffling stones
over the yard one by one, to show she was not done yet, no, yes, she could learn,

with a spirit-level she could do this on her own. *Cheekbones, sandbars,*
her face a delta, patterns of light through leaves through windows,

and far in the distance what does she see, riverbeds running to a river mouth,
shadow, light, sand streaming towards the sea. A bank of old men sit, half-couth,

listening to the band warm up, as if to ignore something within, a fluttering
like babies growing, or tumours, pains of the heart or lung, blown bellies
    pushing

up at their chests so it's hard to breathe or sing, all except Kenneth that is,
light little Kenneth, the slippers of an acrobat flitting beneath him as he runs in,

out, in with smiles and plates, keeping plates spinning for Noreen's sake,
washing pots, making jokes, and for a kiss from the women, giving out birthday
    cake.

*

The women are feathered,
shamans of the afternoon.
Have you ever seen such food
they say, sandwiches, meat, fruit
a feast of love and sacrifice
laid out on trestles. *Oh Noreen*!
It could be heads with apples
served *out there* in the dappled
spring, in the almost-summer
woods, *outside outside*
in the speckled afternoon.

*

Noreen's unwell, but keeping it hidden
with make-up, lies and derivatives of opium.
        Between smiles and belly-laughs she teeters
        with fun, following the twists of her tri-walker
and warmly, welcoming us in, *weave weave
the shadow the sunlight*, aglitter with sarcasm

when Kenneth goes wrong, though shimmering
for the band, remembering herself
singing *Summertime*, and *A Nightingale
Sang* before her voice was ruined.
No-one is looking, so she disappears
to the bathroom to breathe and hold on
to the basin. *Lass, lift up thine eyes!* She repairs
her slap, winks at the mirror, and reels
out again, jangling bangles like a tambourine
man and humming the band's next show-tune.

*

A girl, perhaps eighteen, brings Noreen gifts
and birthday greetings.
Slim in her rumple-clean clothes, we notice
the ease of her black-and-grey clothes,
thrown on, designed
un-designed.

*Isn't she gorgeous Noreen!
She's got your eyes. Do you remember, your Dusty
ash-blonde beehive!* Fashion
out and in, high, low
bootcut jeans, small
earrings, huge,
painted, unpainted,
festooned skin.

*

Outside the leaves shake

patterns of light and shadow
sweeping the lawn
And the old women say *oh*
love to each other
in their cerises and peacock green.

*

Joyce asks me to take Sybil's arm
and smile into her eyes. Sybil says *Shirley*
is it really you? Are we
all right, love?
Where do we go?
Look, here come the young ones –
their skin, their hair!
You're not Shirley.
Where's Shirley?
Too plain, too spare.
Shirley, could I have been beautiful once?
I don't know now –
and outside the slow
   slow-motion
     explosions
       of leaf-
          green
            beech
are coming to perfection and Spring
streams through the window.
Joyce takes Sybil by the hand
and sits her down.

*

Cynthia is up. She is pointing with her manicure

at the copse, she is Boadicea in the sun.
With her crimson lips she is oracle, priestess.
Grace she says, *look, the leaves are weeping,*
Look Grace, the running light!

*

Irene has her glamour on, her white teeth in.
With her sisters she has come to honour

one of their own, Noreen, brave, almost intact
and eighty today. They could be peacocks

calling over a lake, peacocks scrying
the past, the future, *vivify vivify!*

They see flitterings in the trees outside
the stippled leaves, the freckled light,

and delve the wood. Gazers, diviners
holding the secrets of oldwomanhood.

*

Suffering quietly, the men sit, *light running like water*
though leaves through windows
and over their eyes.
They could be a shelf of amphorae,
quite still, and full of regret

all except Kenneth that is, who won't let himself think
what's the point for heaven's sake.
He wheels in and out, serving
cake, till Donald's cadenza stops him
mid-step. *Oh sweet Orpheus!*

Part-time member of the concert-band

Donald has come to play the lady's birthday tunes.
Today he feels at one
with his trombone, plays solo, swoops
soars, climbs,
holds a note, holds it, ecstasy

blowing away his years,
all eighty-nine of them
all *eighty bleeding nine and*
still working!
Kenneth proclaims *Donald*
is King!

                                   *

Grace breathes *No*, and rises:
her bright nails flicker
over her perm. *Here's to Noreen!*
she cries, crying the cry
of a peregrine falcon.
Here's to you my friend, Empress
in your sequins
hip hip,
          hip hip,
our Queen, our Queen ......

MASS

In his *History of Aeronautics* E Charles Vivian
declared the weight of a humming bird

to be one drachm   a condor four stone
Last year little hen   when you were nine

you were as heavy in my arms as a newborn
Now I hardly notice your weight
        Unbodied almost
            air more than bone   more
                    feather than meat
                        spirit
        still quick
            still quick still
                bright   you are
                                leaf-light

                                        leaf

                                                light

'THE HEARTS OF THESE WORDS'

The hearts of these words are bruised but also their eyes
receive without judgement resigned as birds
unable to rise from water because of a net
because of waterlogged wings

thee
elm
caulk
bedlam
mud
moil
fallow
o-o
utter
sump
deoch-an-doris
thither
hither
wait
stammer
weight
mummer
omma
immer
talitha
talitha koum

WATCHING OVER YOU IN CLINICAL LIGHT

the inexplicable lions come to mind
    how they swung out of the houses
on that ruined street   their nonchalant lope
as if off to play soccer   then mosey on to the pub
not knowing the end of this road
was where they'd detonate
landmines   left for *the terrorists*

Then the elephant that leaned against the hut like some winter-dog
wanting a home   or heat
          I can hear breathing
          the sound of skin
          scraping wall something
          infinitely patient
          vast in its kneeling
          breath like a stranded
          whale
          like a whale

Then the infestations
when we first arrived in this watery place
        how they rose up in the floods
between floorboards   roosted at windows   ladybirds
moths slugs the flies
    and once that ganglion of hornets   out of the blue

last month you insisted you'd heard a mosquito
     but you were wrong
the rash on your body was the unknown
second bacterium

so however we look at it
we are back in such days

I pack for the road between visits
    your narrow hat
your outdoor greatcoat
    compass   torch   nutty brown
boots

your mother's teapot is wrapped in the blanket
two passports   harmonica   *Leaves of Grass*

In my own rucksack   tea and sardines
    a packaway boat and the capes I've made from the blue tarpaulin
easy to unfold in rain

        So you see there's nothing to worry about

you can rest
    breathe out
breathe in   they say it's hard work   elephantine
roughness

            like a whale

breathe   please

I thought just now you were trying to rise
                to signal through the screen
you wanted to touch
    to hold my face to your face   so we could go
    backward

September smell of apples
        January
smell of snow
the smell of plums   of hay that August
so you can think   so you can think   how did we
cross the sea   how did we hide from the farmer
        how did you
                take me into your arms
        so that we became milk

HERD

SLIPPING OF LIGHT

The sun comes out halfway down the sky, stroking sheep
half asleep in their wool, birds, the last creatures awake
in trees, the trees, the sides of hills, as if this is it
and there's no more time. I am missing you, old ones,
the way you could light or dim the room. I haven't told you
I am discovering it's all the same, a whole new country
this tenderness. Driving north, I watch the afternoon
slide sidewards over Yorkshire's used earth. The sun
is old and no longer lights from without. Instead it seems
to feel its way, igniting torches stored inside
sheep, birds, trees, the hill, so they might be
their own lamps. This I believe, is similar to love.

At night, I feel at home
with these hills. They lie down beside me like cattle
in the dirt they are in.

I call them in the dark and they shift
like cattle do,
Sanga cows, or Highland cows, like kine, like kin.

I know I'm not the only one.
Secretly at night, they settle down by each of us,
keep us warm, and in.

These are the names I give them: Kith. Oom.
Sough. Ox.
Gert. Brute. Tlou. Seth. Olifant Cough. Olifant Bone.

NEW HOUSE

Wild, last night. Gale force eight. Sykeside,
I remember, half-pulled from dream
by the clamour of unknown trees at war,
different ginnels rattling between the houses.
Deep down, another sound: subterra.

It could have been the mantle's struck
bell, rocks falling, or roots, hoof, blood,
something visceral, a cow giving birth to calf
after calf in a cave underground. Sound
stopped. It must have stopped. I slept.

This morning's white: I don't know where
I am. The whole herd's gone. Mist bright
and silent. Seems I could walk through
haze, in any direction, and arrive at a coast.
Who untethered the mountains?

SHEEP

The hill could be sky,
with its snow.

The sky does nothing,
nothing.

Under my feet the road is narrow,
reels forth frozen

to the horizon
gaily, darkly, as if remembering

a lorry full of boys going to war. Why
do I laugh out loud

when a sheep
comes into view

galloping behind the sound
of its own clattering?

Something about that sheep is awry –
it runs towards me

sheeplike, but unsheeplike.
Wool distracted, dainty high heels

undone, horn without thought,
shoved on. Here it comes

hurtling down as if it might jump
into my arms.

The intimacy of terror.
It's not going to stop.

Those lake eyes say
oh god oh god

the hill's collapsed! Or
Please! Someone, anyone,

tell me, tell me
what is my name?

VACATION

Wrapped in plastic macs or merino
snow gear, we know this isn't real
except in the dark. It's a history park
with weather. But still – give thanks:
to enter is to remember long-lost
creatures, our own shapes
lumbering and whispering like mothers
in the night, and discover what we know
and miss about ancestors, the body,

the pelted soul, and so give rest
to our first-born selves, worn out
with unsuitability and bewilderment,
while the cadet in our mind's
paper boat, continues to paddle
furiously – expert, fit – keeping
the whole show upright, alone,
and dodging debris in the flooded
urban culverts of the facts. Valiant.

LOSING THE SWAN

I noticed bright things on the ground:
mushrooms, lichen, small wet plants
with frills. Bunting. After nine years, today
was the day America left Iraq. Climbing
through trees to snow, I felt air suddenly

open: a propulsion over my head, swan
so close I glimpsed the sinews joining
wings to body, saw them stretch, bunch,
stretch out, the lengthening pits of axillae.
Size of a small goat, that torso.

There was the whirr, the industry of wings,
but I swear I also heard the swan's beak
sawing at air like a handheld saw
would do, as if it had to, like a birth,
to make room in the world for itself,

for the narrow head, the body, heavy
as a child, wings splayed wide as arms.
Who but a pilot could have imagined
the obstinacy, the intransigence of air?
The swan flew over Grasmere

straight towards the snows of Heron Pike.
I waited for the turn, its wheel back
across the water. It was now or never,
or so it seemed, but at that moment,
a fighter-jet corkscrewed in, split

second before its sound, and slit the day.
When I looked again I'd lost the swan.
Had it sensed the coming of the plane,
and fled? Or hid? Or doubled-back
perhaps in play, heralding with glee

the arrival of a strange familiar, unknown
family? Or was it all coincidence?
Did the swan, despite the sound,
calmly dip its wing at the perfect time
to turn, and land beside its mate

gliding behind the island? I still don't know.
Snow began to fall so I walked back.
From every vantage point I looked,
I checked, but saw no swan upon the lake.
I turned to magic. Perhaps it never landed,

but in some snow-pact with Heron Pike
kept on going, kamikaze pilot, scout
for all the forced-out disappearing things,
to fly its density of down and hammer-heart
straight into the opening mountain.

DUNMAIL RAISE

The Atlantic falls on us, has for days. I abandon Grasmere's field,
the drowned meadow of its lake, and drive to Keswick.
On Dunmail Raise the sun comes out. I am waylaid
by colour, oxblood, russet; wet, dead bracken laid out like worsted,

each crease between the fells, a wide or narrow seam of white.
I stop, park up, get out. The rain begins again, seeping in.
How sad they seem, these hills. Their bodies trudging on, all muscle
shoulder, back; the brunt of stalwart hips, their steadfast necks.

They leave me quiet, like the aftermath of seeing big men felled,
big women brought crashing to their knees and trying to rise, the kind
who till the end defend a cairn, a tarn, a crown, and when all
they know is gone, pray from habit, keep counsel, refuse to cry.

DAWN ON NAB SCAR

I wait in the dark, as if on one foot, tense with the balance of almost
falling, other foot held above the ground. In the minutes before dawn

we are always waiting, stretched between two momentous things.
    Interminable,
and never arriving, the weight of proof has suddenly come, and I realise

I have missed the moment of change – there's already more powder of light
than darkness in the air. Dawn hauls its pale mirror

up through Rydal Water; there are clouds today so I watch the clouds
whitening the lake's surface. Mist in tufts rises like grasses.

Below the house on the farm, a pinkness used to stain the morning mist
above the Broederstroom. Tall grasses in the muddy dam.

On this day, years ago, sixty-nine people murdered at Sharpeville.
Was I implicated? No, yes, where does it begin, and end? A moorhen

is a moorhen, and a coot that swims across glass-still water is also
a pioneer cutting tracks. This one looks as if it wants to separate

water from water, like water is an idea that can be divided from another,
and water will stay separate, grow apart. These are the shapes

the moorhen leaves on the firmament of its lake. Above me, a whole town
wakes: the woodpecker begins its morning routine, opening and closing

the door to its castle, creak, creak, again and again; the little birds whistle
in their swept-clean market place as if no more conflict can ever come,

no bombs, no divided Jerusalem; just there in the distance, spring brightening
the greygreen, green, maroon trees reflected in the water. Two narrow deer

see me and stand, as if they too are reflections of trees with their mossy horns
and legs like the limbs of birches, and they stare, and I stare,

and we slip in and swim, we are lake-ideas, our eyes
pools of brightening water: there is the past and also the future,

something oracular about eyes and water, and if I close my deer-touched eyes,
this road below me could be the road to Woodbush, not a lane on Nab Scar

between White Moss and Grasmere, a lane I'll walk down when I return
for breakfast, and hear on the radio news of another massacre, this time in Syria.

THEOLOGY

for Jenni

Division, absence, loss, separation.
But look Jen, the hills also
   hills moving half-hidden between clouds
      deer half-there half-gone between trees
amongst rain. All are ways (except sometimes)
to today which we've walked in
   tonight, that dark tent
which we'll separately sleep in
   to this minute
      this evening
our temporary home. The rest
   let it all wash downriver to the lake tonight.
Shall we leave it riveted to the water with its nails of starlight
while we drink by the fire and argue the point
of art, not tunneling for once
down that long corridor of despair
contained in every last one of the owl's cries
   not watching the stripped moon rise
from the window
   let's forget the moon's hardness, you say
      do we care, after all this time
that her mysteries have, in our life-times
been taken, and if
the answer is yes, don't let's say yes
   not now, not here. This
      is our one-minute home.

Remember Jen
    and also remind me about the eye being I
       feet the foot, our ear the curled
funnel to the heart, and skin
   this fur, this crust
our bark, our grass.
We are grass!
Are we? you say and disagree
and speak of the Holiness of People
and I tell you of Christian the Lion
and so on and so on till we sleep
happily, and wake, happily
and I run for milk and suddenly see in the morning
the hills kneeling like camels
strayed too far north
   how they wait now for heat
under their moss
    patiently wait
       as if to be ridden.

TAME

How long did it take for the hills
to get used to it? The fencing
of stock, the steady buck or cow-like
buffalo, maddened,
bewildered
at calves being lost, no,
stolen,
the stealing of milk.

The first straight walls
being laid. I think of the farmer,
the waller, the waller's lad, all long dead.
The walls are soft with lichen now,
moss, almost inseparable
from fells.
Not bridles,
brutal,
stone.

The first blossoms are caught in the slow-motion act of bursting
their scabbards. The timid will survive, not these flamboyances

blowing out their innards, shaking out pleats from their whites too early
not to be nipped in the first snip of frost, or unfrocked by the forecast snow.

Today has been full of such sorrows, regrets felt as motes of perfection
breaking, something important breaking, a pod, a contract,

contraction of the heart. If I let myself be flamboyantly open, I feel them
these minuscule mistakes, as well as my own betrayals of the trees,

the birds, the animals. For example, what does it mean to walk in, again
and again, on that young heron? I say walking in, as if the bird is human,

as if its long pond floating with weed and the single-track road laid down
like carpet before it, were the boudoir, the bedroom, the madre

chambre of a tender king in which only the beloved is allowed. A mallard
sieves green with its beak. Everything else is quiet in the aftermath,

outbreathing relief, it is Easter holidays, dusk, and at last the people
go home. Trees wait. Blossoms hold tight. Breath. Beat. All clear.

The woodpecker grinds open its gate and the evening rituals begin:
the deer lips the earth, the mallard dips, the birds call and chunter

as if before doorways of shops, squirrels running along branches
doing chores like the branches are streets and the breeze shaking

brand-new canopies, their signs, new leaves, buds, little white flowers.
And then here I am. Each evening this week I have come, walking into the
   fright

and scattering of animals interrupted while doing their thing, disturbing
the sheep, disturbing everything, especially the young heron who feeds here,

drinks, looks at himself, looks at, and into himself with a concentration
that could be creating. Yesterday when I came, he turned to stone

to wait it out. But with the evening pull of hunger and disappearing
light, at last he risked it, dropped his head to puncture water, sup, sip,

try to concentrate, to ignore me, get the depth back. It didn't work.
He opened wide his resignation, flew. Immediately I missed

the grey-white body, his ponytail, his tribal, inner-city Manchu queue,
I missed the pharaoh eye out-lined in kohl, his neck-tube, narrow,
   vulnerable,

and down the throat-front, the long, punk zip, as if in the past his throat
had been slit, lengthways, then stitched back together in hurry and remorse,
   suture

upon suture in thick black thread. On the dead heron's chest two dreadlocks
of sorrow, the hunter's own hair, I imagined, sewn as a sign, a message

to sisters and brothers to leave this bird alone, he has died once
for no reason, and should not die again. I did not shoot or even throw a
   stone,

but here I was nonetheless, staring at his wounds, demanding as my right,
   ownership
of looking, and only now asking, do creatures and trees not need

what I need, to be left alone, to be unseen, sometimes, in
    order to be
themselves, and what I write becomes a question to myself,
    about privacy,

when have I had my allotment of looking, when is it enough?
    And I realise
I am talking of theft. I am talking of the snake at the water
    trough.

THE SWAN'S EGG

From the hill top
we see the swan of winter's dead.
The dreamer couldn't stand it anymore,
cut off its head.

Laid it down
by the swan's docked body, priceless egg,
and crawled back through the tunnel
home to bed.

We all awoke
to birdsong, but what the dreamer saw
was green swan-blood seeping up
through the valley floor.

Children tumbled
into sunshine, played, explored.
Adults smiled at smiling neighbours,
whistling at their chores.

But the dreamer wept
at the window, the greening fields, the trees,
the pointing buds and frothing buds, new
grass, leaves,

then slowly climbed
the hill-top, dreamed arm-wide wings, and flew.
We bow our heads and wear dark coats,
swear we never knew.

But all summer long
we watch the dappled cygnet grow,
and know by November it will be white, snow white,
sooth-saying snow.

IT'S SPRING

I

I can hear the hills going waaah waaah waaah.
Lay your ear. Underneath the grass
and bare stones, haunches flex
tense, begin their slow stamp
tempo tempo tempo, dance
faster, dance louder
waaah waaah
waaah
it's Spring!

II

and the birch trees slip their roots and spin
and I see white legs and the geese bark
and beech trees pin maroon to the sky
and oak sprouts yellow and the geese bark
and Rydal sprawls and cries with relief
and Grasmere sings to its island drunk
and I watch while swans uplift their wings
leaning back necks and opening beaks
as if to yodel the black and white twins
of labouring sheep labouring sheep
and the hills roar and the geese bark
frogs purr and the geese bark
geese bark geese bark . . . . . .

THE OPENING MOUNTAIN

AFTER READING YOUR MANUSCRIPT UNDER THE SYCAMORE TREE IN MAY

for Helen

Leaf husks
                     everywhere
no   the word's too dry like crusts or
biscuits   let's call them   mother-
petals   new-leaf   mother-
petals
long   soft
   their throat-pink fading at the apex
                           to palest
primrose

Suddenly everywhere   pocks
                     specks
           stipples
on the sky   drifting sideways
             adrift as children
     moving through afternoons

Petals land   neck-first
on the chicken-coop roof
      the path
    my hair   and a sharp gust
shakes   the canopies
   the sycamore   shakes
its leaves   leaves shake off
their petals and petals
   fly out like water   flying
from a shaking dog

All this   so I almost missed
the leaves of your manuscript
                              taking off
from under my glasses left on the bench

                    the whole
        white
                              bright
            flock

lifting and wheeling as if they sensed
the warm days coming
                          and it was time

It took me a while   to find and collect
the pages caught in brambles and weeds
one splayed in the water trough
                              three caged in
the leaves of the birch   another
        perched on the elbow of a sycamore
branch   and balanced
            as if it might
                    teeter
                          over the edge and

            launch

an innocent out in rough air again
                following the dim unraveling
instinct
home

PERHAPS NARCISSUS

Perhaps Narcissus was misconstrued
      and what he gazed at was the world
upside down, fragile, easily disturbed.

      Perhaps Narcissus fell in love
with idea made image. Suddenly perceived
      his pool both mirrored life, and lived.

Perhaps he saw in the still water
      of some creek or watercourse or quiet delta,
two things at once: the muddy bottom of a river

      and his reflected face. Leaves, roots, murk
underwater stalks of willow-moss or gypsywort,
      the busy stir of ponds (shrimp, newt, perch

and there the shadow of the perch far down)
      while on the surface, a simultaneous screen
of cloud and sky, trees, rushes, reeds all trembling

      on the river's skin and yes, his own face,
silver as he stretched out to wash or fish, Narcissus
      – framed by willow, violets, burning iris –

lit by this thought: *Perhaps pictures in this pool*
      are what's most real, imperfect as they are, frail,
dual, and like thought itself, able to unfurl, unfurl, unfurl –

THERE IS THIS

for Mair; and for Robert

You place flowers each day in the window
flowers you have chosen for surprise or colour
or the reverie
in the fall of their stalks.

They are balanced and touched by the light
making the dullest lucent,
each flower perfect
in its steady moment of unknowing

I think of vulnerable necks, people
absorbed as if sewing at dusk
with one lamp on,
or reading a book by a window.

Whenever I enter the room, I notice the flowers
and am taken by the hand,
led by a sister
through uncut fields in June

and I remember my brother, our legs
swishing and wet from the morning grasses
and my brother is saying,
look – there is this

and this, and this, and this.

TURNER

for Sheila

Each day this week
as the lights switch on
in maple and beech

you bring home a bowl
from the workshop.
Handcupped

they warm as you oil them,
like brightening
slow-oven fruit.

Autumn's loss and blaze
distilled, compressed
in the bowls you turn,

and you slow down
the fall, make leaf-light
substance.

POETRY READING 14 NOVEMBER 2019

i.m. Mark Hinchliffe

You came in while Anthony spoke of Rilke and Mahler
– not you of course, but the shape of you slowly

wide as a cupboard, making your way to a chair
and from there you listened like you always listen

hearing as if from below, from a sweet-water well
or cave in a rocky hill, your hare-ear attending

as wintering bears might attend, eyes closed
to hearken, homing-in on *inside* rather than *out* – no –

half-hearken, half-dream there's something that must
be remembered, be knitted together, bodies

of love, grief, song – and you lift your head, seem to
see all the souls amongst us, your eyes have changed,

deep yellow now, the colour of November
beech leaves bright with rain –

DEERSUDDENLY

deersuddenly
there

two / no / three launching
to get away hsh
hsh hsh

leapline interrupted
by trees beech / no / birch
between us and light
stammering
like shutters / no / film clips
clp

deersuddenly
stopped

in the pixilation
and confusion of brush
they pretend to be memories

images intuited
in black and white
passengers on a platform
silent with suitcases
portmanteaux
valises
no / suitcases and trunks
there they go / vaulting
landscape / no / let them be
landscape / no /

carriages of trains
flickering behind landscape / no /
trees / behind trees
clp

now they are trees
trees or stones
with height and weight
greenwood columns say
in chapels built for a green man
. a green man
    no /piskies / no /
        picts / no /
            celts oh
deergone

deergone

nnn
nnn
nnn the wind
its empty coat hung
in the trees

GO-BETWEEN

Who stands at the gate?
I have tripped and trudged through mist
to approach the farm from a lane
coming over the tops.
I recognise nothing, but imagine
a town in the distance
– Denholme, Stainland, Halifax –
black crust
cresting the snowy dip.

And there you are old stag,
animal head on human body
human neck.
A body that's undernourished
and to me, looks hurt.
I can't pinpoint what's scarred
exactly, blemished, unwashed,
sternum scooped in and undeclared
by cloth or blue tattoo.

But those animal antlers
stand crown-proud
and divide the wind
making it sing and sing
vowel-sounds
finding the scallops
of horn, scapulas
spatulas, spoons, sibilance
following branch and twig
until all around is clamour and hiss
Whose voices ring in the wind today?

Whose voices cry?
Whose lie?
Whose sigh?
Go-between, tell me
what do they say?

air

air

AIR

ah

    aer

               ruah

          aane

    anjn

                     anda

             animm

        anima

animal

        the animating vital principal
        in woman man and animal

                        spiritus spirare espirit
                              aspire respire

960 breaths an hour
        ve   *va*
vetru   *vindra*
  feth
gwynt

                         vint

            windaz

wawan

     wander

         windan

     wind

there's a whole grey drove ~~herd hjorth~~ that comes from the west/
south west

and shoals of summer breezes ~~breath-az breath-az~~ from the south/
south east

sometimes a beast of a southerly ~~beste bête~~ brings
thunder/ heat

or ice-winds ~~ulfa ulfa ulv~~
howl down from the north /north east.

Creatures that breathe:

dheusom

          deuzam
       dius
            deor
    diar
                tior
      tier
dyr

      dier

         deer

    dear

THE PASSING

Something has to break from the day
        and sob
trees are empty   elk
summoned to encircle the house
        balance
dusk on their antlers

But when darkness touches the ground
                they will gallop away
in an eddy of leaves   and tomorrow
        winter
                will burst in on us
in all its snowy-coloured skins

MIDNIGHT, BELTANE, SOYLAND MOOR

Ruche after ruche night is gathering, cloud piled
over the moor, dim scone
for a moon, flat pallor lidding Huddersfield, Halifax
Manchester.

Up here it's cold. Dead sheep, winter –
keeps dragging back
to unfinished December
out of kilter. On the skyline, pylons. Skeletal
goddesses they hum
as if a sun-surge has come and gone
or something huge and clandestine is passing down lines
and they listen in
O soldiers of ruins make preparation

Here where not much is alive, and moor-grass
stunned with electricity and longevities
of snow, I realize I am intent on making up stories. I find kith
in things: tractors, signposts, an analog radio. How gaunt
these pylons are, meanings accrue,
they are almost old enough now to be prophets.
Fact is, no cattle careened
out of their barns today, no cows tossed ribbons like horses
or blithely lifted hooves
to cross the grass as if they were calves again. Beltane,
and fields remain empty. Where do we go?
The sea-starved sea. These days, screens
are our lamps, yet tonight I want oceans,
oracles stinking of goats
in the dark, ribald women
who fly.

On the skyline, pylons. Tension
a kind of desire. Ambiguous
as they are, for a moment I imagine
they could show us how: *Elbow. Knee. Elbow. Hah!*
Akimbo sisters!
Give birth. Show your steel
farthingales. Hoist skirts. Pant. Point
your six arms downwards,
wake the earth. Hoist!
Hoist!
Cavort!

On the skyline, pylons. Clouds eke
and open. Let me be cheerful. Look a star is coming out, and another
each with a secret that science can't fathom,
not really, not yet,
and while the sound up here is not
the sound of the sea, it could be, almost, this traffic
coming and going from the M62 to the M60.

GREEN

A lover comes out of the woods in April
smelling of root and cloud

Last night we met
under the dusky lamp
of copper beech.

I warned her of the hive in my head.
She said *Let it swarm* and we lay down
amongst islands of wild garlic ready
to be bruised and hogged.

Waiting for calm, I asked what made her
wake.
                              The pain she said.
Hatchlings of snake.
They hurtle through phloem
burst bark
    make buds
        dissolve into blossom

I look up at the leaf silhouettes
and things fall into place.

Only last week, I thought I saw locusts
breaking out of their pods
unpleating damp wings
on those sycamore twigs.

We are all displaced my lover said.

I collect litters of Spring as she sleeps
make circular patterns of batteries, wrappers,
plastic. Then lying beside her
I wait for bluebells
to neon under the moon

I wonder when she'll be gone.

Just before dawn she begins to lay leaves
over my body. They feel cool and fine as baby
green skin. *You're see-through* she says.
Inside your chrysalis I can tell you're a moth
trying to be born. But there'll be traffic
and war when you wake.

AUGURS

At first they depended on birds
but birds came and went

        so they attended to gardens
        until drought

They leaned faces on trees
that had shaded great grandmothers

        When summer didn't return
        they knew time for trees was over

In droves they decamped to the rocks
the shining cliffs

        to search stacked drawers of limestone
        or sense with feet

basalt, batholith clocks, imponderable
oracles of granite

        Now they've been found along tidelines,
        strewn, staring up at the night

the future impenetrable behind them
history gazing back.

THE RISING

The roof of the distant house is still attached,
lashed down with tarp and rope
by the woman who floated past
on a section of road.

Now fieldlakes are sea. I watch wavelets
lap at tip-toey hooves of sheep and goats
on archipelagos. Tail to tail
they stand stock-still and stare

at this tree, at the house, at the ridge
in the distance that hides the farm.
Only when their hocks go down do they bleat.
The bleating goes on.

The man who thought he was alone in my tree
croons a song of comfort. A tenor.
He sings to the beasts in a tongue I don't know
but it could be Hebrew. Perhaps he's a cantor.

He reminds me of my mother so I lift my voice
in her home language, the Arabic
I hardly know. She'd say I'm tone-deaf
and godless, but I harmonise as well as I can.

He looks up at my branch, shock in his eyes,
raises arms in the rain. I think he weeps.
We both sing louder. And an answer shrieks
from the hill. Vixen. Kits. Tod.

Dogs howl back from the house. A woman
leans from an attic window, yowling cat
under her arm, chicken shrill on her shoulder.
The woman is waving. She sings

of waters that stood above mountains,
covers of the deep flung out like garments,
a God who came to rebuke the waters,
and the waters fled, they fled.

A bellowing stag on a knoll to the east.
I hear scream of hare and keckering
badger. Moles and beetles join in
with squeals of weasel, squirrel, rat

even dumb worms open their mouths
to mouth at capsizing frogs
and otters that mew from a channel.
Then the sounding of cattle.

It is duduk and shofar, calling
to the planet's diaspora, and I see
herds from the milkfarm in silhouette
amass on the hill. A lion from the moor zoo

roars his answer, and there is sweetness
in the sound of cow and lion lowing together.
I think of my lover and I miss her.
And just as the noise reaches crescendo

birds rise up like bodhisattvas,
and all things with wings strain skyward as one
to lift up the world. Crows, bees, peregrines,
pulling skyward with bats and swans

and on the backs of hawks, the little things
singing and singing, mayfly, crane-fly, wren,
and high up, a harrier, and there a dove,
I'm certain I'm looking at a collared dove,

and I turn to ask the man reciting kaddish
when I realize that he and the sheep
have gone quiet, the goats are swimming
in silent circles, and water pulls at my hips.

POSSIBILITY OF HORSES

BALANCE

Walking away from the town,
I passed a half-ploughed field,
furrows turning inside out and black
behind a new tractor. The driver smiled,
waved, and I waved back

watching him tilt
the balance of light. In the unharrowed part
sun rilled between bleached-out oat-stalks,
its silvery influx running like water.
Crows were landing to feed there.

On the way back from my walk,
the tractor was stuck on the field's far side,
marooned in the dusk. As if it had foundered,
was a wrecked boat leaning
under the weight of birds

hundreds of them now,
crows mostly, flowing over
the tractor's cabin or hovering above it
waiting to land, occupying the green
metal wheel-guards

while other birds ransacked
islands of unploughed ground.
I called out. I couldn't see the driver
anywhere. *Calm yourself* I thought.
Home-time, that's all.

So I too made my way home, and left the crows
trawling for seeds in their ragged lines,
while smaller birds bobbed
between the great sunk wheels,
shrieking *Corvus! Corvus!*

PAUSE

Driving north towards the first snows
I see the moon's blue hare
      balance on its ears.
Except for a ridge of cloud
the sky is clear
      suspended
waiting for its morning
happening
         selah.

      Nnnnn the sky half-belonging
      to the night nnnnn the sky reaching up
      on tiptoe for the day
everything today explained by sky
its bank of deep blue becoming
pink without a threshold
strip of violet. Should there
not be violet?
Not today
         selah.

Radio alert. Soon a gale
will blow from Russia
and the tight contours of a front
make mountain maps of storm
though now it's bone-china
dawn give thanks
         selah.

Give thanks the trees are still as cakes
whole canopies dipped in sugar in the night

and in the light
remaining lit.

Close-up
             etched rooks.

Claw-lock.
             Zip-breast

                          black anorak
                          of wings.
                          Tucked.

Sheep tucked.

                          Each
                          an isolate

             motionless
             in its cumulus.

And I too
bring my car
to a stop
         selah.

                 Looking up
                 I see the outline of the moon
                 fading in the early light.
                 Blue hare hangs yet
                 could break through
                 at any time twisting
                 upright from its caul
                 to escape and haunch away

before the onslaught
of the storm

give thanks.

And if it proves too late selah for that
might it fall unseen to earth
defrost in its plastic bag
    inert
knuckle knurl selah
grey blue
selah

selah

till the coming of the night?

WHIT MONDAY, HALIFAX

The hard town undoes
the buttons of its shirt

bares its stone ribs
to blossom in the dawn

and at five am
on the bank holiday

before night-shift workers
from the Nestle factory

make their way home
I look down from the hill and see it

lying there half asleep naked
its people cradled in its arms

and the sun

MORNING LIES ALONG THE HILL

Morning lies along the hill, lover
waking slowly
half-folded in cloud.

Purple and orange haze
balanced on the tips
of Rough Hey wood

has disappeared overnight.
Now trees rediscover
the greens they can be.

I think of you waking
in another house
sunlight your body

stored all through
this bright and lamenting spring
coming off you

a light of your own
that you rest in
and will leave behind.

If I could touch it
the light would be almost
warm as you

following shape
close to the shapes
you have been

as you slept.
Like leaves becoming
just above the woods.

TODAY IS BLUE LIKE BLUE USED TO BE

I could almost ignore the fields
pale as sponges, the exhausted trees
stunned but upright.

Horses stand side-on to the sun
either asleep or watching steam rise
the whitish grass.

Still as tables laid with cloth
and bowls of warm food, they don't move a muscle.
They don't want to ruin it.

Flowers are tougher
than they look. Crocuses push up their soft torpedoes
while daffodils yell at the sun.

Building continues.
Bony crow-nests shake high up, twig-knots
loud on the sky. Trees will remember.

It's the beech trees gingerly
hanging out blossom of grey tatty plastic
I want to talk to.

Perhaps they and the horses
understand facts I've only half-grasped.
Being human I hope

it might go something like this
When we are finished, first them then us
or maybe the other way round

there won't be redemption
exactly, but days of a kind, ugly
and heavenly as this.

WHAT WE KNOW

The horses have gone, and come, and gone.
On this farm they bloomed
brief as arums.

We laid our foreheads against their flanks
and breathed in the beginnings of ourselves
haysweet and saltsweat
and the afternoon smell of hot wood.

Our old man reported
that what had returned to him
was the shape of horses
forming through mist.
They had stood there like nurses
waiting for stretchers coming in from the fields.

He said as he passed they forgave him.
They forgave us all he said.
They lowered their lordly muzzles
and breathed
and now he could forgive us also.

For what, I asked. But these days I wonder
if the possibility of horses
is almost extinct in us.
Through all the poison
and cleanliness
it is hard to be calm.

THIS MAY MORNING

The sun and the dead.
The milkman clock.
On the whispering radio
politics.
Outside, a cat

stalks through vetch.
Buttercups. Quaking-grass.
Son without work.
Everything is attached
to its own leaning shadow.

Alone in your bones
you wake. Our sunlit bed.
This May morning
your years lie on you
strange, heavy coat.

TODAY, DESPITE THE BRISK WEST WIND

these turbines stand exhausted
as if they've praised and praised the Lord
waved and waved at passing planes
and still remain unrescued

walking down the corridor past all the doors, the doors shut,
as faces deeply asleep are shut, like hospitals in the night,
lit, drugged by the light, washed out, snuffed out by flat quiet light
as if morning could never come again, which it won't, not the same,
not quite the same as this one morning in my mind, cool and pale
and calm, the sky so high that the fine pencil lines of pink resound
with the high strung silence, its beauty a mesosphere of silence
above that quiet dawn grass, strange and covered with dew, white
in the way moonlight on grass can be white, colourless and other
and holding its breath, as if breathing would be a path, the trace
of a ghost, a progress of footprints appearing through mist, or one
by one, green, wet, bending the grass and unpeeling themselves
heel, toe, heel, black as the holes on water.

Who wouldn't want to be the walker who first walked across
this expanse, but before I could reach the bluegum tree in the garden
all those years ago, it occurred to me that perhaps I was spoiling my own
immense morning. Why would I remember this? Is it imagining you confined
within a well-walked, strip-lit corridor, searching for a view, a door, the one
amongst the many shut, brown doors you might recognise as distinctive,
a low anxiety settled in your chest, or is it in my chest, that this may be
the passage in which we all get lost, perhaps it won't end, or suddenly
it will end, so the only place to go is onward, towards the lapping
glare of light that seems to smear out everything ahead, that light
lapping like a lake on this corridor-floor, the shore of an implacable
lake a few steps in front, always in front, and taking me forward,
leaving no footprints, these, my baffled, slippered feet.

SUMMER

Here, summer has always been young
a promise, a longhaired swimmer.

Hard to believe in breath
holding this long. Many

have drowned. But at dawn one morning,
water will shatter –

a seal a woman an otter a man
gulping in blue air, there

in the blue skin of beauty, hair streaming,
hosanna lung-full and golden

for all of us. We'll open
our eyes and inhale morning,

minds averted, please for one day
from all that is spoiled, become fewer

become few or unable
to break through the mud.

We'll lift sternums like wishbones
up to the sky, unbandage, sigh

awake again to our shapes
and lean across

space, cold body
that has lain too long between us

and touch
touch, shaking hands

with neighbours who will sidle out later
with backpacks and bikes

faces uncovered, grief
and bare limbs shy as ours in the sun.

THE ESCAPE

And the sky opened   laid its wings flat   settling in on wind
for the long flight seaward   Everything today has an iota
of other tucked into its body   becoming or releasing itself
taijitu   We have all lost something   We drive east
out of these vales   their sadness unspeaking green   deep
steep roads leading upward   Colour changes colour
slides down to its horizontals   Width   The width of it
lamina after lamina   Low tide   Freshwater marsh
salt-marsh   mud   mud-banks   sand-banks   the sea

*

On the vertical over sand   a black and white cyclone
    kittiwakes   terns   little terns all shrieking
Isak   Isak which means *he will laugh*

A tangle of children   twist and shriek   fall and
    rise in a channel between sandbanks

while a boy with olive green shorts throws back his head
    dances on a hip of mud   ankles and feet   damson
and gleaming   is it hiphop or laughter   perhaps he is *Felix*

*

Your hair in this light looks silver   glistens like white
in the waves   Gulls and terns twist inside out   curved

sharp   white now black   weaving a glittery basket
Beyond the sand   there are fish in dark waters

resting in spheres as if they   are in baskets
Sea too is resting   suspended between breaths though

channels at our feet keep running and running
bringing gospel to layers of ocean awaiting their turn

*

Shadows   Three clouds staining acres of water

*

Belly half-moon   an infant in turquoise stamps
and stamps the slush   Splish splosh   asqueal

with his own magnificence   he has spied
two bright garnets   crabs scuttling past and tips

into a run   becomes unconquerable   Odin
out on the wild hunt shaking a spade at his quarry

His dad tears after him   hands low and outstretched
for catching his lamb   From a different picnic

three small girls   almost identical in periwinkle
join in the chase   The crabs reach the bank and burrow

One bout to the crabs   Now it's hunting for treasure
Boy warrior   *Afrah*   *Farrah*   and *Felisha*

*

On the leeward side of a dune a ragged plain   lilac
  violet   *I think you say*   *it's sea lavender*

Your lips taste of salt   Next to the path
is samphire   We taste it   Walk north

*

Seaward   birds funnel and bark   Landward
  sea buckthorn   Long leaves of olivey grey
  Thorns   white needles   Marram
Dune grass   Reed sweet-grass   Pendulous
sedge   We follow the samphire

*

A tern gazes down at the water she stands in
a puddle left by the tide   *Thulani*
meaning *peaceful*   I imagine she knows herself

sees that her long   yellow-red legs are becoming
their reflection   and her beak is a yellow-red thorn

Beyond her   turbines reach out to a place between
Dogger Bank and Holland   They don't lean but
they could   there's longing in those arms going nowhere

*

In the sky above ditches crossing at rightangles
   a kestrel oscillates   plummets   coming up
empty   He hangs on muscle in his quivering
   basket of air   puritan cartographer
memorising ideas of good   or wicked cities
Lets call him *Michael*   meaning *who is like God*

                              *

We pass a milestone   Ochre lichen growing on the granite
a perforated circle   almost perfect   Its four gaps fan

north   south   east   west   making milestone
godstone   a celtic cross of yellow cadmium

                              *

Sea-buckthorn has many names   *Hippophae*
meaning *shining horse*   Sandthorn   Seaberry
Long thorned Sallowthorn   Thorns like
stalled turbines   though sharper and in miniature

                              *

On the beach a grandmother   white hair floating
   crimson sundress tucked into knickers   Her legs

wide and planted are two brown pillars that today
   won't be knocked down by the tide   She leans

over the *littl'un*   lannels him in lotion   *rub a dub*
dub and together   they build castles in the draining sand

A young woman calls   *Joyce*   *Joyce*   *I've found*
Asher's armbands   Asher's armbands are turquoise

*

Far out   strips and stria   Purple   Indigo   Ochre
patina on patina   A whole translucent geology

cross-sections of light and water   Damson   Ink
Olive   Yellow   The purple is mud from the mudflats

*

I leave you with your new binoculars   walk to the edge
of the sea   Waves flop over like rows of white knitting

If I don't move   there's no one but me touching feet
with my bubbling shadow   If I was the last in the world

I think I would talk to shadows   the innocent ones
tall and hardly there   calm monks of dusk and dawn

flawed human-size ones of mid morning and mid afternoon
with whom I would gossip and vacillate   doing my best

to forget how I tramp on the silent dense shadow of noon
        enraged   and so often flailing

*

        Sky slides into the sea

*

At my feet a littoral convoy   sanderlings crying   *quick*
quick quick   Speed of a speeded up cine   I can hardly see legs

but they are making a dash for it   sea-edge is terror
and also the border to freedom   In their own motorboats

they switch the electric anxiety-switch   on   off   on
then dart back to the mirror-wet sand   Sanderlings

running and running   all dreams of themselves cradled
in pale holdalls held under their bodies until they reach dry land

                              *

        Dark kelp on the tideline like smashed up wings

                              *

I turn   You have lowered your binoculars   wave
I wave back   High cloud   Fine manes of shining horses

*

We pass two people   asleep in each others arms
bodies at rest in their papoose of touch   her thigh
    over his calf   his shirt rucked up
showing a hand-width   spilling of tummy
They are *David* and *Cerys* meaning *beloved*

                              *

We walk on to find fish-and-chips
You are humming   We play name that tune
and I see colours are different
     there are azure stripes out to sea
          and the position of purple and pink
               are changing places

ST OSWALD'S CHURCH
Grasmere

Layers. Priors and befores in the walls, storage of prayer, but also something earlier, shifting strata of human, crow, auroch-cow – patience like the first act of building, sweat and wattle, ivy-sap plaited by builder into pilings and branch-beams, the new-cut laths.

Shelter for all. Pebble. Fur. Straw. Curraghs of mud stuffed in and scraped. Dung sorrel-sweet, stuffed in and scraped, slate-scraped, smoothed to a finish. The burnish of ordure and rubbing along. Shepherd, stock-stealer, nomad, farmer. Later the mystics

though the heart of this church is a byre. Functional, it has the herder's temporary architecture, wide as a house for wintering beasts and tenders of beasts. Pasture, valley, lake. Afterthought – a good place. Burgeoned with faith and the habit of gathering, built-on to, built-up on, consecrated by a saint, it crumbles and remains permanent. And under the sacrament, under services, tours, meditations of historians and Sunday church-goers, under each flagstone walked shiny by feet, thud, shift, faraway lowing,

close-up pelt-press, stink-fleece, animal-heat, the walls of a stable, a Mercian fold. Always going on, this bringing in. And there half-hidden in the rushes of the stalls, a woman and a man. Imagine. She's thin. He has dirt smeared on his cheek. Daub

has spattered their garments, stained palms, hands to the wrists, the soles and tops of their feet. In her brown arms, she holds a child. Exhausted, peaceful as trees, man and woman sleep. The child opens its eyes. Stares into our eyes. Amused. Awake.

Greylag
The words in italics are Dutch: gaan means 'go', vandaag means 'today', veranderen means 'change'.

Kestrel
Luft and Lug both mean 'Air' (in German and Afrikaans respectively), Lig means 'Light' in Afrikaans, Luch means 'Mouse' in Irish

Wren
roitelet and dreoilin are words for 'wren', in French and Irish respectively

The hearts of these words
   o-o : a bird whose last song was heard in 1987 and is probably extinct
   deoch-an-doris: means 'one for the road'. A Gaelic term (literally 'Drink of the door') for the practice of offering a guest a final drink before the journey home.
   omma: According to Wikipedia Omma is a genus of beetle in the family Ommatidae, and is an example of a 'living fossil'.
   immer: means 'always' in German
   talitha koum: means 'young girl, arise' and is quoted in Mark's Gospel (Mark 5:41). Jesus was said to have resurrected a dead child with these words.

Before the Map
Oom means 'Uncle' (Afrikaans)
Tlou and Olifant mean 'Elephant' in SeSotho and Afrikaans respectively

Air

The words in italics are etymological roots or sources for the following connected words: air, breath, animal, deer, dear, spirit, wind, wander, herd, beast, wolf.

Midnight, Beltane, Soyland Moor

The sea-starved sea: this is a reference to a line from the poem 'A Crazed Girl' by W.B. Yeats. The actual line is: *But sang, 'O sea-starved, hungry sea.'*

Pause

Selah: The actual meaning of the word selah is not quite clear but it occurs in the Psalms and probably comes from the Hebrew. It is thought to indicate a musical direction for a pause, or a break in the singing, which is how it is used here, but has various other interesting interpretations.

ACKNOWLEDGEMENTS

Thanks are due to to the editors of the *The Compass Magazine*, *The Fortnightly Review*, *The North*, *PN Review*, *Pennine Platform*, *Shearsman Magazine*, the anthology *This Place I Know* (Handstand Press, 2018). Thanks too to the following blogs, John Foggin's The Great Fogginzo's Cobweb, and Kim Moore: Poetry.

Many thanks and acknowledgements to the Wordsworth Trust, and to the Hawthornden Retreat. They both provided opportunities for exceptional residencies for which I feel most grateful.

There is a community of outstanding local and Northern poets who together make a fabric that is holding and supportive. Sometimes this manifests through discussion and comradeship, sometimes through providing each other with direct responses to each others' work, and often by individuals generously making wonderful poetry events happen so we can all participate. I cannot name them all, but amongst the people who make things happen are Stephanie Bowgett, Sarah Corbett, Anthony Costello, Julia Deakin, John Duffy, Steve Ely, John Foggin, Bob Horne, Ian Humphries, Sarah Hymas, Nigel King, Kim Moore, Peter Riley, Peter Spafford. Warmest thanks also to all the members of the Albert Poets, Poety Club, Puzzle Poets, Writing Group, Elmet Trust and The Bookcase.

I am grateful to Jenni Molloy for the inspiration of her music and creativity, and to Sheila Tilmouth for the inspiration of her visual art. Heartfelt thanks also to Tim Moss, Anne Landsman, Helen Tookey, Rob Hale, Albert Potrony, and

Olwen May for their feedback and encouragement. Also to Andrew Forster for his facilitative and thoughtful editing of the pamphlet *Herd*.

Particular thanks are due to Judith Willson for the sustenance of our discussions, the acuity of her reading, and all her help, not least in arranging the order of this book.

I am very grateful to all at Carcanet, especially to John McAuliffe for his steady, insightful and attentive editing, to Andrew Latimer for his typesetting and beautiful cover design, and to Michael Schmidt for the invaluable space he continues to keep open for poetry, and for his support of my better work. Thanks too to Jazmine Linklater and Alan Brenik and everyone on the Carcanet team.

And finally, my thanks to Sheila Kershaw, who professes to know nothing about poetry, but is my first and often wisest reader.